FABULOUS FASHION INVENTIONS

LAURA HAMILTON WAXMAN

LERNER PUBLICATIONS COMPANY
MINNEAPOLIS

For Yana, my
lovable little
fashionista

Copyright © 2014 by Lerner Publishing Group, Inc.

Lerner Publications Company
A division of Lerner Publishing Group, Inc.
241 First Avenue North
Minneapolis, MN 55401 U.S.A.

Website address: www.lernerbooks.com

Library of Congress Cataloging-in-Publication Data

Waxman, Laura Hamilton.
Fabulous fashion inventions /
by Laura Hamilton Waxman.
pages   cm. — (Awesome inventions you use every day)
Includes index.
ISBN 978–1–4677–1093–0 (lib. bdg. : alk. paper)
ISBN 978–1–4677–1646–8 (eBook)
1. Fashion—History—Juvenile literature. 2. Inventions—
History—Juvenile literature. I. Title.
TT504.W39 2014
746.9'2—dc23   2012048774

Manufactured in the United States of America
1 – BP – 7/15/13

CONTENTS

INTRODUCTION

WHAT'S IN YOUR CLOSET?

What's hangin' on your hangers and chillin' in your dresser? The latest fashions? Or are you a comfy jeans-and-T-shirt kind of kid? What you wear can tell people a lot about you. But clothing also has a more practical job. It protects you from all kinds of weather. And it helps you to stay modest when you'd rather not bare all. These basic human needs are what made people invent clothing in the first place.

Our early ancestors didn't have malls or even sewing machines. Everything they wore, they made by hand. Feeling cold? Perhaps you'd slip on a warm fur cape. Hot? You'd likely wear a simple covering of animal skin—or nothing at all!

In modern times, machines made fancier clothing possible. Take the 1800s. Men wore silk ties, tall hats, and coats with long tails. Women wore poufy dresses over hoopskirts, lace head coverings, and leather gloves. And kids? They wore mini versions of the same thing! It took a long time to get dressed, that's for sure.

You wear clothing that's a lot more comfortable, right? And it probably takes you only a few minutes to dress. Your favorite outfit may be a tube skirt and a tank top. Or maybe a pair of shorts and a basic T.

No matter what, each fashion invention has a great story behind it. Read on to hear some of these surprising and often inspiring tales.

Do you have trouble deciding what to wear? Consider yourself lucky. For much of history, people had only two or three sets of clothing.

Two fashionable women pose for a photo in the late 1890s.

BLUE JEANS

Blue jeans are an American classic. But did you know an immigrant from Europe made them famous? That immigrant was Levi Strauss. He came to the United States from Bavaria (that's in Germany) in 1847 when he was a teenager. Sixteen years later, he opened his own business in California. Strauss sold work clothes, tools, and other supplies to gold miners.

One of Strauss's customers was a tailor in neighboring Nevada. Jacob Davis bought tough, long-lasting cloth from Strauss. Davis used it to design super-sturdy work pants. Davis's pants had something special—copper rivets. Davis sewed these small bolts into the seams of pockets. The rivets stopped the seams from tearing apart. Workers loved his long-lasting pants. He couldn't make them fast enough.

Davis wanted to patent his design. But he didn't want to pay the hefty sixty-eight-dollar patent fee. In 1873 he asked Strauss a life-changing question: would Strauss like to go into the pants business with him? Strauss knew a good offer when he heard one. He said yes and paid for the patent. Soon after, Levi Strauss & Co. began producing jeans made from blue denim. Known as Levi's, the jeans sold like hotcakes. Over time, they made Strauss a millionaire.

Workers loved Levi's. But to most people, denims were totally uncool. Laborers and prisoners wore them—not people of fashion. Teenagers changed that in the 1940s and the 1950s. For them, wearing jeans meant being tough and rebellious. It meant looking like heartthrob U.S. movie stars such as Marlon Brando and James Dean. By the end of the 1950s, the sale of Levi's jeans had nearly tripled. Since then, blue jeans have become popular around the world.

Gold miners, such as these men in the 1850s, often wore blue jeans.

James Dean (LEFT) helped popularize blue jeans in the 1950s.

THE BRA

Before the bra, most women wore a corset. This stiff undergarment was made of cloth such as cotton or silk. Harmless, right? Except it had thin strips of bone or steel (called stays) inside. The whole thing was held together by cloth laces. By pulling on the laces, a woman could squeeze in her waist and shape her bust. But corsets were so tight that they shoved around a woman's internal organs. Ouch! Not to mention that it was hard to breathe in one. Seriously unfun.

By the early 1900s, women were fed up with painful corsets. Some inventive people tried to design a more comfy undergarment. One of them was Mary Phelps Jacob from New York.

According to one story, Jacob was at a ball one evening in 1910 when inspiration struck. She didn't like the way her corset covered up too much of her neckline. So she pulled off the undergarment right then and there! Later, at home, she did some major brainstorming. What she eventually came up with was a bra made from two handkerchiefs and some ribbon. She showed it to her women friends, and they loved it. In fact, they each wanted a bra of their own. Jacob patented her invention in 1914 and started selling it. But she was a society lady, not a businesswoman. She quickly lost interest in the bra business.

Soon Jacob sold her patent to the Warner Brothers Corset Company for $1,500. Over the next three years, the company made $15 million selling bras. Other companies began making bras too. To many women, bras became a symbol of their growing freedom and equality in society. By the 1920s, the bra had replaced the corset for good.

Harper's Bazaar for April 1957

I dreamed I led the Easter Parade in my
maidenform
Chansonette

I captured the essence of Spring in Chansonette, America's most popular brassiere. Fabulously flattering circular spoke stitching giving rounder, more captivating curves.

From the best stores and shops ... in white poplin at 17/6

Pre-lude—
A touch of pure genius

Pure genius this contour band! Curving up snugly between the cups it gives you a completely new kind of "under-and-up" lift! Today, discover Pre-lude. In flower-fresh white embroidered cotton at 17/6 and in snow-light embroidered nylon taffeta at 21/-.

BOTH STYLES
A cup 32"–38"
B cup 32"–40"
C cup 32"–42"
(even sizes)

MAIDENFORM (LONDON) LTD. 68 OXFORD STREET, L[...]

This Maidenform bra ad is from 1957.

A corset drastically changed the shape of a woman's bust and waist.

ADULT WOMEN AREN'T THE ONLY ONES WHO WEAR BRAS. Many younger girls do too. The first bra for girls was invented in the 1950s. It was known as a training bra. (Do girls really need practice to wear a bra?) Unlike women's bras of the time, which often had stiff cups, the training bra was softer and didn't have cups.

BUTTONS

Buttons are one of the world's most useful clothing fasteners. They keep our shirts, cardigans, and pants closed. But the first buttons didn't do any of that.

In ancient times, people fastened clothing with pins made of shell, bone, and other natural materials. Folks in ancient India and China may have invented buttons. They just forgot one thing—buttonholes. Those first buttons didn't line up in rows. And they didn't hold anything together. They were used only to decorate clothes. By the 1200s, people were wearing decorative buttons to show off their place in society. If you were rich, your buttons were made of sapphire, gold, or other precious materials. If you were poor, you wore plain cloth or thread buttons. In fact, in some places it was illegal for common people to wear fancy buttons.

Buttons got their big break in the 1700s. That's when factories began producing a lot of cheap buttons. Many were cut from huge sheets of metal. Others were made from animal horns, hoofs, and shells. Unlike earlier buttons, these buttons actually had a job.

Factory-made buttons began fastening everything from soldiers' uniforms to men's trousers. Soon enough, they appeared on women's clothing too. They showed off a woman's curves by making dresses and undergarments fit snugly. Meanwhile, wealthy people in the 1700s and the 1800s spent a fortune on hand-made decorative buttons. Buttons painted with tiny landscapes or portraits were very trendy.

Nowadays, most buttons are made of plastic or wood. But they're still pretty. In fact, did you know that button artists make buttons that people collect? These are some of the most beautiful buttons of all!

A BUTTON CRAZE SPREAD ACROSS EUROPE DURING THE 1600S. And the finest, most expensive buttons came from France. No one spent more on those buttons than France's King Louis XIV (below). Rumor has it that this bling-loving ruler spent millions of dollars on buttons!

The modern plastic button was introduced in the mid-1900s.

BASEBALL HAT

The UPS delivery guy wears a brown one. Nicki Minaj wears a pink one. You might even wear one. It's a baseball hat. And it covers millions of people's heads around the globe.

Baseball hats haven't been around forever. American baseball became popular in the 1840s. Those early ballplayers wore straw hats—or no hats at all. The baseball hat wasn't  invented until 1860. And it didn't look at all like it does today. Most baseball hats were curved around the sides and flat on top. They also had no team symbol or name on the front.

Slowly, the baseball hat took on a rounder shape. Then, in 1901, the Detroit Tigers began sewing its team symbol onto its caps. Other teams liked the idea and copied it.

In 1903 the Spaulding sporting goods company designed the Philadelphia Style cap. It had a visor stitched to the front to shield players' eyes from the sun. The rest of the cap was sewn together from six panels, or sections. The hat also had airholes to keep hot heads cool.

That basic baseball hat hasn't changed much since then. It became fashionable in the United States in the mid-1900s. Over time, that fashion spread to many other countries around the globe. These days, the baseball hat industry is going strong. It sells $2 billon to $3 billion worth of baseball caps each year. That's a lot of hats!

Sam Crawford wore a Philadelphia style cap with a Tigers team symbol on it in 1909.

Nicki Minaj's bright pink baseball cap is all about style.

BAT-AND-BALL GAMES PROBABLY GOT THEIR START THOUSANDS OF YEARS AGO in ancient Egypt. The games made their way to England and then to the United States. The first official American baseball game took place in 1846 in New York. The game quickly became popular across the United States. By the 1850s, baseball was being called the country's national pastime.

SWIMSUITS

Imagine swimming in a thick linen gown and tights. Now imagine heavy disks sewn into the hem to weigh the gown down. Sound like fun?

For a long time, European and American bathing suits weren't much good for swimming. That's because showing skin in public was seriously uncool—or even illegal!

By the early 1900s, that trend had changed for men. They could wear tank tops and shorts to sunbathe and to swim. Women weren't so lucky. Their bathing dresses had gotten a little shorter. But they still weighed around 22 pounds (10 kilograms) when wet. Try swimming in that!

Then Carl Jantzen came along. He co-owned a struggling knitwear company in Portland, Oregon. In the early 1900s, a customer asked Jantzen to make a knitted swimsuit that would be tight but stretchy. Jantzen experimented. The result was a knitted men's swimsuit that became an almost instant hit.

Jantzen made a similar swimsuit for women. But he had to convince them to buy it. So he plastered newspapers and magazines with his ads. "No need to waste your energy dragging a wrinkled suit through the water," one ad said. "You can slip through the waves as smoothly in a Jantzen as in your own skin." His ads worked, and women all across the country began to wear his swimsuits.

Over time, swimsuits were made from more waterproof and formfitting materials. They also grew smaller. By the 1930s, American men were going topless in the water. And in 1946, the first women's bikini came out in Paris, France. At first, the skimpy swimsuit shocked Americans. But by the 1960s, the bikini had become all the rage. On modern beaches, you'll see everything from one-piece women's suits and bikinis to skimpy men's swimming briefs. Anything goes!

UNDERPANTS

Can you imagine going around without underpants? If you were a girl two hundred years ago, that's exactly what you'd do. In fact, women and girls have gone commando for most of history. Men, on the other hand, haven't been quite as fancy-free.

Someone, somewhere, invented the first loincloth thousands of years ago. This loose covering hung from a man's waist. It kept his private parts . . . well, private. By the 1500s, most European men were wearing some sort of undergarment under their pants. But back then, bathing wasn't high on people's priority lists. Neither was doing the laundry. (*You* try scrubbing all your clothes by hand!) So underpants were pretty important. They protected clothing from dirty, smelly skin. That's why a lot of men's underpants went down below the knee.

People started bathing more in the 1900s, thanks to indoor plumbing. And that's when men said hello to boxer shorts. American soldiers first wore these loose undershorts during World War I (1914–1918). The soldiers liked the boxers so much that they kept buying them after the war. Then, in 1935, a U.S. company began making modern men's briefs. Like boxers, these formfitting underpants were a huge hit. American men bought thirty thousand pairs of briefs in the first three months.

Women wore underskirts for hundreds of years. But underpants? No way. That changed in the 1800s, when underpants became a must for ladies of fashion. At first, women's underpants weren't much different from men's. They went down to the knee or the ankle and were pretty plain. But by the 1920s, they had grown shorter and more frilly. They soon became known as *panties,* and they've kept that name ever since.

This ancient Greek wall painting shows men wearing loincloths.

This ad for women's underwear appeared in Britain in the 1920s.

HANGERS

Hangers are a simple invention with a big job. They keep your clothes neat and wrinkle-free. (Unless, that is, your clothes prefer hanging out in a big pile on your bedroom floor.) Until the early 1900s, most people hung their hats and coats on hooks. People stored other clothes in dressers and tall wooden cabinets called wardrobes. And closets? Forget about it. Without hangers, closets weren't even on people's radar.

The man behind the hanger was a lowly inventor named Albert J. Parkhouse. He worked at Timberlake Wire and Novelty Co. in Jackson, Michigan. One day in 1903, he went to hang his hat and coat on a hook at work. To his dismay, all the hooks were taken. That's when inspiration struck.

Parkhouse grabbed some wire and bent it into two loops— one for each shoulder. Then he attached another hooked piece of wire between the loops. Ta-da! He'd invented the hanger.

Parkhouse's boss liked his hanger idea. *A lot.* He took out dozens of patents on it. That way, no one else could steal the design. Parkhouse's company went on to make a fortune on its "garment hanger." Poor Parkhouse. He didn't get any of that money for himself. He most likely died penniless.

Wooden hangers were popular in the 1950s.

WE ALL KNOW WHO THOMAS JEFFERSON WAS. Author of the Declaration of Independence, the third president of the United States, and... inventor of the wooden hanger? Well, not quite. But he did invent a spinning clothing rack! His pants, coats, and other clothes folded neatly over rods attached around a pole. To find a piece of clothing, our clever president simply turned the pole.

Modern hangers are often plastic and come in many colors.

VELCRO

Some inventions are inspired in the most unlikely ways. For Swiss inventor George de Mestral, a simple walk in the woods led to the creation of Velcro.

De Mestral went on that leisurely walk in 1941. Along the way, he and his dog got into some sticky burrs. These spiky balls are parts of plants. And they're really hard to remove from clothes and fur. Most people would have been seriously annoyed. But not de Mestral. The burrs gave him an idea. He wanted to make a fastener that held just as tightly.

De Mestral examined the burrs closely under a microscope. He discovered that tiny hooks cover the sticky balls. These hooks loop onto clothing fibers—and don't let go. De Mestral set out to copy those tiny hooks, but it wasn't easy. Luckily, he had something in common with the burrs: stick-to-itiveness. He refused to give up.

Nearly ten years later, de Mestral had reached his goal. His invention used two materials that worked together. One was covered with tiny hooks. The other had tiny loops. When

pressed together, the two materials stuck. De Mestral decided to name his invention *Velcro*. The *vel* comes from the word *velvet*. The *cro* comes from *crochet*, which means "hook" in French. De Mestral got a patent for his invention in 1955. Five years later, factories worldwide were making 60 million yards (55 million meters) of Velcro each year. That's enough to wrap around Earth nearly 1.5 times. And that was just the beginning. Talk about an invention that stuck around!

VELCRO SEEMS TO BE EVERYWHERE. Even the National Aeronautics and Space Administration (NASA) uses Velcro. The sticky material fastens uniforms (below). It also keeps tools, utensils, and other objects from floating around in space. One astronaut even brought a Velcro chess set to the International Space Station!

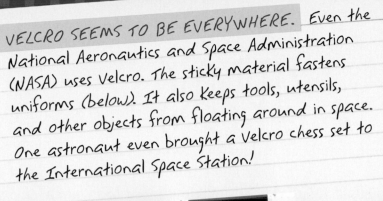

This photo of Velcro is magnified two hundred times.

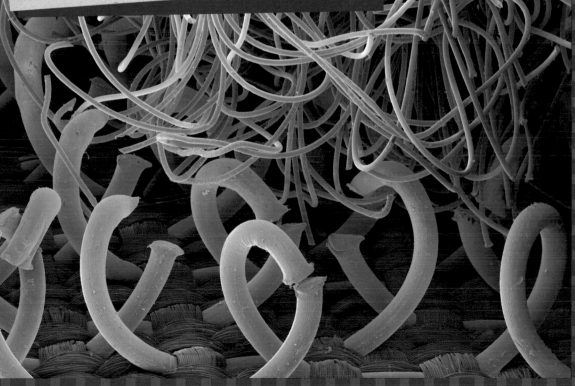

ZIPPERS

Have you ever had a simple idea that turns out to be not so simple? That was true for Witcomb L. Judson. This engineer from Chicago, Illinois, had a dream. He wanted to invent a better way for women to fasten their boots.

In the 1890s, boots were *the* shoe to wear. Most fastened with long laces or rows of tiny buttons. Opening and closing them was a real chore. Judson invented a slider. It could open and close a row of hooks on boots. He called it the clasp locker.

But the clasp locker got stuck a lot. And the row of hooks burst open at the worst times. Judson kept trying to improve his invention. But he died before he could find a good solution. One of his company's employees was a Swedish American man named Gideon Sundback. Sundback was determined to make the clasp locker work. In 1913, five years after Judson's death, Sundblack invented a new slider. This one opened and closed a row of interlocking metal teeth. Sundback's slider worked like a charm.

At first, clothing producers weren't interested. They couldn't figure out what to do with the thing. The only taker was a company that made uniforms for the U.S. Navy. The company bought a bunch of Sundback's sliders for flying suits. In 1923 another company bought them for rain boots. By the 1930s, other clothing manufacturers had seen the light. They began sewing zippers into their products. They liked the way Sundback's slider zipped up and down so easily. And that's how the name *zipper* came to be.

THESE DAYS, MOST ZIPPERS ARE MADE BY A JAPANESE COMPANY. The YKK Group has zipper factories in fifty-two countries. Its U.S. factory produces 1,200 miles (1,900 kilometers) of zipper every day!

Zippers are used both to close clothes and just for decoration.

SHOES

In 2012 Darlene Flynn from California broke a world record. She owned 16,400 shoes and shoe-related items! For people like her, shoes are a fashion obsession. But they started out as protection for cold feet.

The earliest footwear was invented about fifty thousand years ago in snowy northern climates. Around that time, humans were probably wrapping their feet in furry animal skins. The skin and fur kept feet warm and dry. That idea led to the first shoe ten thousand to twenty thousand years later. That's when Native Americans were sewing animal skins into moccasins. Soft-soled moccasins allowed them to quietly sneak up on enemies or prey. Moccasins with stiff, leather soles protected people's feet on rough terrain.

Sandals were invented around the same time. They worked well for people who lived in warmer places such as Africa, the Middle East, and southern Europe and Asia. The soles were made of leather, woven plant matter, wood, and metal. Some of the earliest sandals were flip-flops! They had one strap that fit between the toes. Other sandals had straps that went over the foot or around the calf.

Boots are another ancient type of shoe. The first boots were made of animal skins. For extra warmth, people lined them with fur or other soft materials. In ancient Greece and Rome, soldiers wore leather boots into battle. Heeled boots were also invented in ancient times for horse riders. The heel kept a rider's feet from sliding out of stirrups. Today everyone from firefighters and motorcycle riders to fashionistas wears boots!

The high heel is another shoe that's been around a long time. It got its start in France in the 1500s. At first, it wasn't a shoe for women. Nope, the first high heels were for rich dudes! The French king and his noblemen wore them as a sign of their high rank. In fact, the term *well-heeled* came to mean "a person of wealth." It didn't take long for noblewomen to want a piece of the high-heeled action. By the 1600s, the high heel craze had swept across Europe. High heels were fashionable for men and women through the 1700s. Men stopped wearing them by the late 1800s. But they've been a popular women's shoe ever since. Can you imagine Lady Gaga without high heels?

 One of the most modern shoes is the sneaker. It didn't come along until the 1900s. It all started when a British shoe company invented soft rubber soles in the late 1800s. Before that, shoes had hard soles. Shoes with rubber soles were light and comfortable. They were also quiet. They didn't click and clack on the floor the way hard soles did.

In about 1916, the U.S. Rubber shoe company invented a shoe with a rubber sole and a canvas top. The company called its shoes Keds. But an advertising agent for the company called them sneakers. He noticed that people could sneak around in them without being heard. Sneakers have come a long way since then. Thanks to rappers, actors, and pop stars, they're a fashion phenomenon. (Think superstar Justin Bieber and his colorful high-tops.) Top-of-the-line sneakers cost a bundle too. The Nike brand's most expensive sneakers cost thousands of dollars. Whether you wear sandals, heels, or high-tech sneakers, shoes are one great invention.

Lady Gaga sports a pair of her trademark high heels in 2012.

STILETTOS WERE INVENTED IN THE 1950s. These shoes have super-high heels. They're named after the stiletto dagger. Like this dagger, the heel of a stiletto shoe is long and skinny and is made from steel. You don't want to get stepped on by that!

This 1959 ad for Keds shows many types of rubber-soled shoes.

Summertime U.S.A. begins with   U.S. KEDS...for everybody

Keds
The Shoe of Champions

Teens, tots, moms, pops, everybody loves U. S. Keds for lots of reasons. Keds look so nice. They feel so good. They wear so well. And kids will tell you Keds run faster.
The truth is genuine Keds are built over lasts that are scientifically shaped to fit active feet. Unlike ordinary sneakers, Keds are

made with shockproof arch cushions like this ⟶ to absorb the jolts and jars of running and jumping.
And Keds wear longer. Soles and uppers are permanently bonded together. You can keep them clean in your washing machine. Genuine Keds are easy to identify. Always look for the blue label.

US United States Rubber

ELASTIC

Think of a world without elastic. How would you keep your undies and socks up? And what would stop your gym shorts from falling down? Thanks to Thomas Hancock and Charles Macintosh, you don't have to find out.

In the 1820s, these two British guys were busy making stretchy bands for clothing. The bands were sewn into shoulder straps, corsets, and the wristbands on gloves. To make the bands, the men molded natural rubber into thin, elastic strips. The natural rubber came from South America. But it had a major problem. In cold weather, it got hard and brittle. On hot days, it went all gooey and sticky.

In the United States, Charles Goodyear was also experimenting with rubber. In 1839 he heated up rubber on his kitchen stove. Then he mixed in sulfur, another natural material. (Yum-yum!) He soon discovered that heat and sulfur made the rubber stronger. The end result was vulcanized rubber. Unlike natural rubber, it stayed stretchy and kept its shape.

Goodyear tried to sell his product in the United States. But no one was buying. So he hit up Hancock and Macintosh. Sneaky Hancock went behind Goodyear's back and made his own vulcanized rubber. Then Hancock took out the first patent on the process, just days before Goodyear did.

Hancock and Macintosh used vulcanized rubber to make elastic—and a lot of money. These days, most elastic is made with synthetic, or human-made, rubber. But it's still suuuuuper stretchy! And it still does its thing—keeping up your pants!

Rubber, like the kind in this rubber band, is the basis for elastic.

THOMAS HANCOCK MADE A FORTUNE SELLING RUBBER PRODUCTS. Charles Macintosh made a name for himself too. He used rubber to invent the first raincoat, known as the Macintosh. Charles Goodyear never got rich. But his name lives on in the Goodyear Tire Company. Its cofounder, Frank A. Seiberling, named the company after the American inventor in 1898.

Elastic can be found in suspenders (LEFT), waistbands, and stretchy fabrics.

GLOSSARY

corset: a stiff, tight-fitting undergarment that shapes a woman's waist and bust

denim: a tough cotton material used in jeans

loincloth: a piece of clothing that hangs down from the waist to cover the lower body

moccasins: shoes sewn from animal skins. Native Americans first invented moccasins.

patent: an official document giving an inventor the sole right to make or sell a particular invention

rivet: a small metal fastener

stiletto: a type of high heel with a long, skinny steel heel

vulcanized rubber: rubber that is heated with chemicals to make it stronger and stretchier

wardrobe: a tall wooden cabinet with drawers and shelves for storing clothes

FURTHER INFORMATION

Bata Shoe Museum
   http://www.batashoemuseum.ca
   Everything you wanted to know about shoes can be found at this
   fun website.

Behnke, Alison. *Does a Ten-Gallon Hat Really Hold Ten Gallons? And
   Other Questions about Fashion.* Minneapolis: Lerner Publications,
   2011. Brides always wear white. Wearing a hat indoors can make
   you bald. Learn whether these and other common beliefs about
   fashion are really true in this book from the Is That a Fact? series.

———. *The Little Black Dress and Zoot Suits.* Minneapolis: Twenty-First
   Century Books, 2012. Read about American fashions of the 1930s,
   the 1940s, and the 1950s. This book is part of a larger fashion
   series called Dressing a Nation that looks at fashion in the United
   States through the ages.

Eighteen-Century Clothing
   http://www.history.org/history/clothing/intro/index.cfm
   Check out this site to learn about what people wore in the
   1700s—and what their dolls wore too!

History of Clothes
   http://library.thinkquest.org/05aug/00726/index_files/Page1187.htm
   Visit this site to learn about the beginnings of clothing in Africa.

Inventors and Inventions
   http://www.kidskonnect.com/subject-index/15-science/86-
   inventors-a-inventions.html
   This kid-friendly site is loaded with informational links related
   to inventions and inventors.

Kyi, Tanya Lloyd. *The Lowdown on Denim.* Toronto: Annick Press, 2011.
   Learn more about the history of jeans.

Niven, Felicia Lowenstein. *Fabulous Fashions of the 1960s.*
   Berkeley Heights, NJ: Enslow, 2012.
   This title in the Fabulous Fashions series takes you on a
   journey through clothing styles of the 1960s.

Shaskan, Kathy. *How Underwear Got Under There: A Brief
   History.* New York: Dutton Children's Books, 2007.
   Check out this book to learn all about undies.

INDEX

PHOTO ACKNOWLEDGMENTS

The images in this book are used with the permission of: © Digital Vision/Getty Images, p. 5 (top); © DaZo Vintage Stock Photos/Images.com/CORBIS, p. 5 (bottom); Library of Congress pp. 7 (top, LC-USZ62-8197), 13 (top, LC-USZ62-135391); © John Kobal Foundation/MoviePix/Hulton Archive/Getty Images, p. 7 (bottom right); © Alexmax/Dreamstime.com, p. 7 (bottom left); Mary Evans Picture Library/National Magazine Company/Courtesy Everett Collection, p. 9 (top); © CORBIS, p. 9 (middle); © iStockphoto.com/wdstock, pp. 9 (bottom), 11 (top), 13 (bottom), 19 (top right), 21 (top), 23 (top), 27 (top right), 29 (bottom right); © Stefano Bianchetti/CORBIS, p. 11 (middle); © Uokhoj/Dreamstime.com, p. 11 (bottom); © Splash News/CORBIS, p. 13 (middle); © General Photographic Agency/Stringer/Hulton Archive/Getty Images, p. 15; © Marco Simoni/CORBIS, p. 17; Image courtesy of The Advertising Archives, p. 17 (bottom); © George Marks/Stringer/Hulton Archive/Getty Images, p. 19 (top left); © Trgowanlock/Dreamstime.com, p. 19 (bottom); NASA/JSC , p. 21 (middle); © Clouds Hill Imaging Ltd./CORBIS, p. 21 (bottom); © Michael Stewart/WireImage/Getty Images, p. 23 (left); © Sashkinw/Dreamstime.com, p. 23 (right); © Chicago History Museum/Archive Photos/Getty Images, p. 25 (top); © Werner Forman/CORBIS, p. 25 (bottom); © Jun Sato/WireImage/Getty Images, p. 27 (top right); The Granger Collection, New York, p. 27 (bottom); © Echo/Cultura/Getty Images, p. 29 (top); © iStockphoto.com/Voisine , p. 29 (bottom left).

Front cover: © fabioferr/Deposit Photos.

Main body text set in Highlander ITC Std Book 13/16.
Typeface provided by International Typeface Corp.

LERNER e SOURCE™
Expand learning beyond the printed book. Download free, complementary educational resources for this book from our website, www.lerneresource.com.